YORKSHIRE RIDER BUSES

SCOTT POOLE

AMBERLEY

Lower front cover image courtesy of the Malcolm King Collection.

First published 2017

Amberley Publishing
The Hill, Stroud
Gloucestershire, GL5 4EP

www.amberley-books.com

Copyright © Scott Poole, 2017

The right of Scott Poole to be identified as
the Author of this work has been asserted in
accordance with the Copyrights, Designs and
Patents Act 1988.

ISBN 978 1 4456 6904 5 (print)
ISBN 978 1 4456 6905 2 (ebook)

British Library Cataloguing in Publication Data.
A catalogue record for this book is available from
the British Library.

Origination by Amberley Publishing.
Printed in the UK.

Contents

Foreword

Transport has played an important part in everyday life in West Yorkshire, beginning with humble horse-drawn buses and trams (as well as steam-powered trams) transporting folk around the area. Huddersfield Corporation can lay claim to the first electric tram operation in the country, which opened in 1883. Soon Leeds, Bradford and Halifax followed the tramway operation, with trolleybuses from 1911. Bradford operated trolleybuses until late March 1972; Huddersfield withdrew its trolleybuses during 1969, while Leeds curtailed its trolleybuses in 1928.

The motor bus then began its slow rise within the county and by the 1930s many of the local fleets used AEC Regents, Daimler CVG and Leyland Titans, most with Charles H. Roe bodywork, but many with Metro Cammell and Alexander bodies as well. By the 1960s the rear-engine chassis were slowly beginning to become the vehicles of choice – either the Leyland Atlantean or Daimler Fleetline. As the 1970s arrived the municipal undertakings were nearing the end of days, as the 1968 Transport Act created the new West Yorkshire PTE in 1974. A new Metropolitan County Council was also created at the same time; this body was reasonable for all financial and regional agreements, which included funding for bus and railway services and passenger facilities.

When the 1985 Transport Act, which was normally known as deregulation, became official, bus companies began their opposition to the Act. With this new Act came another Act of Parliament – the collapse of the Metropolitan County Councils, which saw the PTEs lose their legal right to operate a bus service. West Yorkshire PTE developed a new company – Yorkshire Rider – who would operate a bus service from late October 1986.

The former Leeds City Transport headquarters, which became the WYPTE Leeds offices from 1974, saw its final transport name replacing the old Metro Leeds sign and emblem with the new Yorkshire Rider name with 'Moving A-head with' slogan. This building is now a high-class hotel. (**Malcolm King Collection**)

Yorkshire Rider Limited – A History

Yorkshire Rider limited took control of the operation of bus services within West Yorkshire on 26 October 1986. This was part of the deregulation set out by the 1985 Transport Act, which allowed operators to bid for services via the local Passenger Transport Authority and the Transport Commissioner of the area. Notices were issued to all potential operators during 1985, with all details concerning the new act together with details of how to register services, all of which had to be completed by 25 October 1986, otherwise fines would be issued. West Yorkshire Passenger Transport Executive set up the new company of Yorkshire Rider. This new company tendered for all the former PTE services, operational depots and most of the bus fleet. All timetables and promotional details were supplied by Yorkshire Rider and Metro. The West Yorkshire Transport Authority published these on behalf of Rider. Together with Metro, Yorkshire Rider organised a huge publicity campaign with adverts, leaflet drops and newspaper details. On 25 September 1986 a special ceremony was carried out to officially launch the new Yorkshire Rider bus company. This took place outside the civic hall in Leeds with the Lord Mayor, Councillor Mrs R. Lund, breaking a bottle of champagne across the front of 6120 LUG 120P. Also present were local sporting personalities – the 1986 World Snooker champion Joe Johnson and Olympic gold medallist Tessa Sanderson – with Councillor Mr M. Simmons and WYPTE MD and Chief Executive Bill Cottam. After this a cavalcade of preserved vehicles from the West Yorkshire Transport Museum, along with 1712, 1603, 5505 and 6120 all painted into the new Yorkshire Rider liveries, travelled around Leeds before venturing towards Bradford. The following day the event visited Halifax and Huddersfield.

Two Leyland Atlanteans were used for livery trials behind closed doors. The new bus livery was unveiled during late September 1986, with various buses used. Brilliant green and jonquil were chosen, with fleetname and district in red. The district name was last used in 1977, before the PTE dropped these in favour of a simple livery application. After deregulation, the fleet was still in the Verona green and Buttermilk PTE livery, but by late 1988 most were painted in the Yorkshire Rider livery. The coaching arm of Yorkshire Rider was also given a new livery. The Gold Rider fleet was painted in an overall oatmeal colour, with black skirt and red-and-gold stylised 'YR' logo. The minibuses were painted mainly in the jonquil colour with green bands and red 'Micro Rider' fleetnames. The early livery had a little bear with the word magic in a bubble.

West Yorkshire PTE withdrew a large selection of new and old buses on 25 October 1986, but before deregulation the PTE purchased several Dormobile and Carlyle-bodied Freight Rover Sherpa minibuses. The following Leyland Olympians were withdrawn from the West Yorkshire PTE fleet: 5001–17, 5049, 5050, 5056–64, 5066–76, 5078–80. These were purchased through a leasing scheme, as were Alexander MCW Metrobuses 7512–19 and MCW Metrobuses Mk II 7539 & 7540. The Olympians were sold to various operators, including Blackpool Transport, Metro Bus of Orpington, Wilts & Dorset and China Motor Bus, while some of the Metrobuses were sold to Stevenson's of Uttoxeter or London Buses.

Yorkshire Rider purchased fifty-three Daimler/Leyland Fleetlines and twenty-three Leyland Atlanteans via Kirkby Central, a dealer. These were former Greater Manchester Transport buses;

three had Park Royal bodies while the rest had Northern Counties bodies. The Fleetlines were settled in Halifax and the Atlanteans were used in Leeds. New integral MCW MetroRiders were purchased in 1987–8; some were coach-seated and operated with the Gold Rider coach fleet. Fifty new double-deck buses were purchased in 1988, along with twenty-five integral MCW Metrobuses and twenty-five Northern Counties-bodied Leyland Olympians. The Metrobuses were among the last examples built for Yorkshire Rider, as the MCW owners sold the MCW model rights to Leeds-based Optare during 1990. Also, during 1988, the Yorkshire Rider Limited company became the first PTC to be sold, albeit to management and employees. A selection of the new buses was used to advertise this fact with the slogan '3,500 caring owners'. New buses ordered for delivery during 1989 were five Optare Delta-bodied DAF SB220LC, five Alexander-bodied Scania N113DRBs, and five Northern Counties-bodied N113DRBs. In 1989 Yorkshire Rider purchased the West Yorkshire Road Car Co. The West Yorkshire PTE had wanted to acquire the National Bus Company subsidiaries in 1975, but instead the Metro-National company was set up later in 1978.

From August 1989 to March 1990, buses from both companies were used on all services. Before the sale was completed, various Bristol VRs and Leyland Olympians were moved to the WYRCC operation in exchange for newer Leyland Lynxes. A large selection of Leyland Nationals joined the new fleet. Twelve Leyland Atlanteans with Park Royal bodies were purchased in 1989 from Sovereign Bus & Coach in London. These buses were operated from the WYRCC Leeds depot on Roseville Road; some with West Yorkshire fleetnames over the Rider livery. During 1990, Yorkshire Rider purchased all the York-based operators and formed them into one company as 'York City Rider'. Former AJS company York City & District, along with independent operators Reynard Pullman and Target Travel, were absorbed into the Yorkshire Rider company. During June 1991, the former Leeds depot of Sovereign Street, which was home to the driver training fleet and the minibuses, was closed. The training fleet was transferred to Bramley depot, while the minibuses were moved around the Rider depots. Yorkshire Rider floated on the Stock Exchange in preparation for bidding in the new London service tenders. Around sixty buses and a depot would be required for the services, however the bid was ultimately unsuccessful.

Rider continued to update the bus fleet from 1990 with Scania N113 double- and single-decker buses and Volvo B10B single-deck buses. Twenty-three dealer stock Alexander-bodied Leyland Olympians were acquired in 1990, shared initially between Bradford and Huddersfield, with two used in York for some time on loan. Yorkshire Rider had decided to purchase single-deck buses for delivery during 1993; as mentioned before, these were of Scania and Volvo manufacture. The thirty Volvos were split between Halifax and Huddersfield, while the Scanias were placed in service in Leeds. The new Strider body was designed by Yorkshire Rider and built by Alexander of Falkirk. The former tram depot at Headingley was closed in June 1992; this was first opened in 1874 and occupied by horse-drawn trams, steam trams and electric trams, with motor buses arriving in the 1940s. This depot passed to the PTE in 1974, then to Rider in 1986. Used as a temporary store soon after closure, the site was demolished and rebuilt into housing during the 1990s.

Halifax and Huddersfield operations of Yorkshire Rider were given a boost with the introduction of some new service ideas. The Flagship high-quality services were introduced to give a better service on certain high profile routes. New, cleaner buses were used and drivers with high standards were chosen to start this new drive for more custom on the buses. As the new saloons were purchased the new routes took off, and custom picked up. Further routes were examined for possible upgrade into the Flagship mould. Even some selected vehicles were painted into promotional livery for the new service. Fifteen new Northern Counties low-height-bodied Olympians were delivered in 1994, which were placed into service in Halifax. Ten full-height

Northern Counties Olympians arrived in Bradford during the same period. Five Scania L113CRBs arrived in York in 1994 again with Alexander bodies, while in Leeds six Volvo B6Bs with Alexander Dash bodies arrived. More Scania N113CRB saloons with Alexander Strider bodies arrived in June 1994 – all nineteen painted into the silver and blue SuperBus livery for the guided busway services.

In April 1994, the Bristol-based operator Badgerline acquired the Yorkshire operator, with no immediate change apart from the Badgerline logo in rear windows and wheel arches. During 1995 standard Badgerline single-deck buses in the shape of Plaxton-bodied Verde's and Dennis Darts with Alexander and Plaxton bodies arrived in a new darker green Yorkshire Rider livery. The new Rider district livery featured a darker green overall base livery with a cream band around the lower panels, as well as a lighter green stylised logo and blocks, while the 'R' was also redesigned and the fleetname was now in white. The 108 new single-decker buses arrived painted into the new livery and were placed into service in either Leeds or Huddersfield. However, the First Bus group was created in April 1995 when Grampian Regional Transport merged with Badgerline and, for a time, First was the largest group operator. New ideas were quick to form within the group; a new style fleetname was applied to all buses, and soon 'local identity' liveries were introduced. Bradford reverted to traditional blue livery, but later a two-tone blue livery with red and white bands was used. Calderline, a new name for Halifax, painted its buses in a refreshing white, with blue and yellow relief. Leeds used a white-based scheme with red, yellow and orange bands, upswept towards the rear of the bus. Kingfisher, later Huddersfield, used the Badgerline Rider livery for its buses.

All photographs were taken by the author unless otherwise stated.

5155 was one of five low-height Northern Counties-bodied Leyland Olympians delivered during 1998, looking very smart in the Yorkshire Rider livery. This vehicle had been used on a very special private occasion, with unique Leeds City coat of arms and two Yorkshire Rider fleetnames. The location for this shot is the former Leeds & West Yorkshire PTE Kirkstall Works, which lasted for around 110 years until sold by First. The site has since been demolished to make way for a commercial venture. (**Malcolm King Collection**)

Yorkshire Rider
Limited Buses in Pictures

The Leyland Atlantean with Roe bodywork formed the backbone of the Yorkshire Rider fleet, with 357 examples passing into Rider stock in 1986. Here 6122 heads down Tinshill Lane while working the 96 service to Cookridge.

Former Leeds City Transport Leyland Atlantean 569 pauses in Kirkgate, Leeds, while on the 17 Rodley service in full PTE livery and Yorkshire Rider vinyls.

One of the initial batch of WYPTE Leyland Olympians with Roe bodies, delivered to Bradford district in 1982. 5001–17 were withdrawn during October 1986. 5018–20 were retained by Yorkshire Rider, with 5018 seen here in Halifax during 1995.

Yorkshire Rider continued with a coaching fleet, named Gold Rider, using former metrocoach vehicles. 5507 was new in 1985 as one of five Optare-bodied Leyland Olympians, seen in City Square near Mill Hill Chapel.

1604, a Plaxton-bodied Leyland Tiger coach, new to the PTE's W. R. & P. Bingley fleet in 1983, seen here pausing inside the Bradford Interchange yard.

West Yorkshire PTE and Yorkshire Rider purchased a sizeable fleet of Freight Rover Sherpa minibuses with Carlyle or Dormobile bodies. Pausing between duties in Halifax are 1871 and 1879, in full Microrider livery.

Optare, based at the former Charles H. Roe factory in Cross Gates, Leeds, was created in 1985. The Starrider was built upon a Mercedes-Benz 811D chassis; 2003 was based in Bradford, later moving to Huddersfield and then to Leeds Bramley depot.

During 1992 Yorkshire Rider acquired eight DAF chassis with Hungarian Ikarus bodies, which were placed into service at York. Here 1201 is awaiting departure outside York railway station on the Tang Hall route.

Optare designed the stylish Delta bodywork built on the new DAF SB250LC chassis, five of which arrived in Leeds in 1989. Here 1251 is depicted on Briggate, Leeds, on the 71 Primley Park service.

MCW spent some considerable money creating and designing the integral Metrorider minibus, of which Yorkshire Rider ordered forty examples. 2051 was new in May 1988 and is seen in Ilkley bus station.

A PTE Plaxton-bodied Leyland Leopard, new in 1976 and still in active service some sixteen years later. 8533 departs Huddersfield on the X37 service to Halifax – a fast service between Halifax and Huddersfield, which took twenty minutes in either direction.

Following the 1980 integral MCW Metrobuses were another batch of Metrobuses, but with Alexander of Falkirk bodywork. The 'R' type style was introduced during 1980 as the new modern style for the manufacturer, which was to last until the middle of the 1990s. 7511 to 7520 (UWW511–520X) were delivered in 1982 with allocation to the Leeds Seacroft depot, with the closure of the depot in 1983, 7511–20 and 7501–10 were transferred to Torre Road depot. 7511 is depicted negotiating the Eastgate roundabout while working to Swarcliffe from Tinshill, repainted into Yorkshire Rider livery.

Ford Transit 190D with Dormobile B20F bodywork, number 122. Stands on Briggate, Leeds while operating as a Rider Cub in the blue livery. Luckily these minibuses fought off competition from PMT, who wanted to start a rival service in Leeds. The minibus started with West Yorkshire Road Car in Harrogate as a Hoppa. Later, the bus was transferred to York City; here the bus became part of the Rider fleet in 1990.

1319 was new in 1980 and allocated to Calderdale district, later moving to Leeds in 1984. Here the Leyland National 2 is turning into Vicar Lane from the Headrow, Leeds, working the 19 service to Belle Isle from Roundhay.

During the 1970s West Yorkshire PTE dual sourced between the Atlantean and Fleetline for new vehicles, all with Roe bodies. Here 7022 is paused in Huddersfield collecting passengers for a local service.

7071 is one of twenty-five Northern Counties-bodied Leyland Fleetlines delivered during 1979. The bus is seen awaiting departure on the front line 508 service from Leeds to Halifax.

583, which was ordered by Leeds, arrived into service with the West Yorkshire PTE along with twelve other Roe-bodied Atlanteans. It is seen passing the former Leeds Polytechnic site, now part of the Leeds University campus.

As the coaching market shrank, Yorkshire Rider folded the Gold Rider operation during the early 1990s. Here Leyland Leopard 1528 with Plaxton coachwork is seen in full Yorkshire Rider post-1991 saloon livery in Halifax.

1990 brought a new vehicle into the Yorkshire Rider fleet, the Scania N113 series double-deck chassis. 8003 – one of five with Alexander bodywork – is depicted parked in Leeds bus station, looking all fresh into service, working the 33 service to Menston.

Another five Scania N113s arrived with Northern Counties bodywork, with the final one – 8010 – shown paused on Eastgate. The bus is working a former West Yorkshire Road Car service, 733 from Ilkley to Leeds.

During 1989 twenty-four dealer stock Alexander-bodied Leyland Olympians arrived into the Yorkshire Rider fleet. The batch was split between Bradford and Huddersfield; later all were working from Bradford. 5209 is seen brand-new into service in the Interchange at Bradford.

Another of the 1989 Alexander-bodied Olympians is seen working from Huddersfield, fresh into service, working to Longwood.

Coach 1400, a Volvo B10M with Jonckheere coachwork, arrived during April 1988. It won the coach of the year in 1988. The Jet Rider idea was an executive-styled coach with a galley-style kitchen and state-of-the-art multimedia entertainment system, with thirty-two coach seats.

Twenty-five Northern Counties-bodied Leyland Olympians arrived into service at Halifax, all with low-height bodywork, allowing these to work from Todmorden depot. 5174 collects passengers from Keighley on the lengthy Keighley to Huddersfield via Halifax 502 service.

Between August 1989 and March 1990, West Yorkshire Road Car became part of the Yorkshire Rider fleet. The WYRRC and Rider vehicles were being used on various services within the WYRCC network. On 1 April 1990, West Yorkshire Road Car services and buses were absorbed into the Yorkshire Rider fleet. Here Bristol VRT 973 with ECW bodywork is seen in Westgate working the 735 service, with a Black Prince Park Royal Atlantean behind.

July 1990 saw more expansion for Yorkshire Rider with the purchase of the York City & District services, with two other operators also acquired. Former West Yorkshire RCC Bristol VRT 979 is seen turning on Station View with the Grand Hotel and the York walls completing this classic view.

Bristol VRT 988 is seen in Wakefield as part of the W. R. & P Bingley fleet, which operated out of Kingsley depot. The bus is seen working the 498 service to Doncaster during 1992.

During 1988, Yorkshire Rider was purchased by the management and employees, becoming the first former PTE operation to be sold. MCW Metrobus 7600 illustrates the fact of the new status at Otley.

Pudsey bus station has changed over the years; here in this post-1991 view, the station was re-positioned. Here dual-purpose seat Duple-bodied Leyland Tiger saloon 1668 loads up passengers on the ring road service.

Wellington Street in Leeds has seen many changes in traffic priority across the years. Here Atlantean 6117 passes the West Yorkshire RCC bus station. At the time, National Express used the area as a departure point.

As mentioned, Yorkshire Rider purchased the three major York bus operators in July 1990. Former Target Travel Renault-Dodge minibus with Reeve Burgess bodywork 233 pauses on Piccadilly in York.

Prior to the sale of the York City & District operation, Blazefield swapped six Leyland Lynx integral saloons for a selection of Leyland National 2 saloons. Here 332 pauses outside of well-known department store M&S in Piccadilly, York.

1994 saw investment in thirty Volvo B10B-58 Alexander Strider-bodied saloons; this new style was developed by Yorkshire Rider and Alexander of Falkirk. 1020 exits Huddersfield bus station on service 377.

Former Leeds City Transport Roe-bodied Leyland Atlantean 506 collects passengers for the cross-city route 50, serving Horsforth and Seacroft, with extensions at the time to Leeds and Bradford Airport.

During 1987, Yorkshire Rider acquired fifty-three former Greater Manchester standard Fleetlines to supplement the loss of leased vehicles. Here 7208 rests at Halifax bus station, while working the 531 service.

MCW Metrobus 7501 was new in 1980, along with nine other Metrobuses based at Seacroft depot. The bus moved to Torre Road after Seacroft closed in 1983. The bus pauses on Briggate, while working an evening peak-time service.

After acquiring the former West Yorkshire RCC bus service, Yorkshire Rider vehicles ventured beyond traditional PTE boundaries. 5208 parades through spa town and major tourist destination Harrogate, working the 648 service.

Two of the 1988 dealer stock Alexander-bodied Leyland Olympians were transferred across to York for a brief spell. Here 5207 turns into Station View, York, while working the 7 service, during July 1990.

West Yorkshire RCC acquired the Leyland National integral saloon via the National Bus Company's vehicle policy. Here 1341 exits the old-style Leeds bus station heading out to Middleton.

Yorkshire Rider took into stock the Mk II MCW Metrobuses for continued service. 7557 is parked on City Square, awaiting a turn on the 83 Garforth service. This area of Leeds has been transformed into a pedestrianised space with bus-only priority zone.

After the West Yorkshire RCC fleet was officially absorbed into the Yorkshire Rider stock, vehicles were transferred across the fleet. 1356 was moved to Huddersfield and is depicted in the town centre working a local service.

A Duple-bodied Leyland Leopard that was new to WYRCC is seen after April 1990 in the new Yorkshire Rider saloon livery. 1550 is awaiting a turn to Otley on the 654 route. This coach was 2603 in the West Yorkshire coach number series and new in 1981.

Yorkshire Rider launched a new standard of service within the Halifax and Huddersfield region of the network. Flagship was brought about to improve service reliability, appearance, better customer relations and dedicated driving staff. This idea was very successful across key routes, which needed much improvement. New buses were also presented for the services. Volvo Olympian 3501 with Northern Counties bodywork was one such vehicle out-shopped in the new flagship style. Here the bus is seen in Leeds working the 508 front-line service between Leeds and Halifax.

Former WYPTE Leyland Olympian/Roe 5082 pauses at the lights at the exit of Huddersfield bus station, ready for another trip out. The bus is promoting the new Flagship standard service for the Halifax and Huddersfield areas.

Fresh out of service with York City & District is this former WYRCC Ford Transit 190D with Dormobile bodywork, 188. Here the minibus is seen on Eastgate roundabout heading out to Halton Moor. Notice the 1991 petrol and diesel prices!

West Yorkshire's Vicar Lane bus station was quite a draw towards the end of operations for the long-established company. Here Bristol VRT/ECW 979 is parked up awaiting a return to Bradford on the 670 service, in company with a Yorkshire Coastliner Olympian.

Bristol VRT/ECW 992 is seen in Ilkley working the 733 service between Leeds and Ilkley via Otley. This bus had been transferred from Wakefield, Kingsley depot, upon sale of the former United Services routes to West Riding.

With the acquisition of the Reynard Pullman operation in July 1990, the Bedford marque made a brief appearance into Yorkshire Rider stock. Here Duple-bodied Bedford YMT 1178 turns out of Piccadilly en-route to Copmanthore.

Yorkshire Rider in 1989 purchased ten Volvo B10M/Plaxton Derwent II saloons equally shared between Halifax and Huddersfield depots. Here Huddersfield-based 1453 is about to return home on the X37 service.

Bradford 5172 – one of twenty-five Northern Counties-bodied Leyland Olympians new in 1988 – awaits departure on a local school service. The whole batch had the YR logo on each seat, with a bright, light interior décor.

Yorkshire Rider also did some work under licence for National Express, as shown by 1424, in full National Express livery in Manchester. 1415, 16, 20–1 and 1423–25 were all detailed for work on National Express route and in the Nat. Ex. livery.

Yorkshire Rider also acquired the two Optare-bodied Leyland Olympians 5146–47 which were specially built as open toppers. Here 5147 departs Leeds Central bus station on the 50A service to Leeds/Bradford Airport, in full discovery bus livery.

Eight new Leyland Tiger/Plaxton Paramount-bodied coaches arrived in 1988 to improve the age profile of the Gold Rider fleet. However, the coaches were soon seeing work on normal stage-carriage services, as here with 1617 on the 556 Oldham service.

As Halifax gained extra Fleetlines in 1988, so Leeds gained twenty-three former Greater Manchester standard Leyland Atlanteans. 6421 is seen about to take a short trip on the main A58 branch road, before heading for Pudsey via the Swinnow area of Leeds.

6424, a Park Royal-bodied Leyland Atlantean, was one of twelve examples purchased from London Sovereign in 1989, built to NBC specification. Here the bus is awaiting a duty on the 733 Leeds to Ilkley service.

West Yorkshire PTE did purchase some Freight Rover Sherpa minibuses, solely for driver training, before the advent of deregulation. Here 1717 rests at the Bradford Interchange in-between training duties; this vehicle was a former Carlyle demonstrator.

Freight Rover Sherpa minibus with Dormobile bodywork 1914 is parked inside Todmorden bus station. 1911–15 were the only minibuses to have dual-purpose seating; all were new in 1987.

This former Dormobile demonstrator minibus was purchased by Yorkshire Rider in September 1987 after being used as a driver trainer. Here as 1941, the minibus is paused on Briggate working a service to Colton.

This former West Yorkshire RCC Plaxton-bodied Leyland Tiger was acquired in 1989 and became 1625 in the Yorkshire Rider fleet. 1625 is seen in Sheffield's Ponds Forge bus station working the White Rose express X33 service.

8009, an Alexander-bodied Scania N113, was one of a selection of Yorkshire Rider vehicles to carry an overall advert for Trophy Bitter. Here the bus is working the 736 to Otley.

MCW Metrobus 7605 pauses on City Square in between duties in a full advert for the Leeds Development Corporation. This organisation transformed ideas into a viable business opportunity from 1988 until around 1995.

Another MCW Metrobus to have an overall advert was 7533, as can be seen of this shot of the bus on Briggate, Leeds.

7520 was one of two Alexander-bodied MCW Metrobuses taken into Yorkshire Rider stock. Both 7511 and 7520 carried over adverts for the pre-paid MetroCard and the Saverstrip multi-journey ticket. 7520 is seen on Vicar Lane while working the 22 to Halton Moor.

Former West Yorkshire RCC ECW-bodied Leyland Olympian 5188 is seen in York, carrying one of the many overall adverts this bus gained. This one is for BBC Radio North Yorkshire.

5193 is seen on Station Rise in York, one of the many former West Yorkshire ECW-bodied Leyland Olympians placed into service at York. Here the bus carries an advert of Minster Windows.

York-based Bristol VRT 746 is seen passing through central York, working the 4 service and wearing an advert for Pilcher Homes. The stunning York Roman wall forms the back drop for the bus.

5119, a former WYPTE Leyland Olympian with Roe bodywork, pauses in Halifax bus station in an overall cream colour base ad for the pre-paid MetroCard, with a former West Yorkshire Plaxton-bodied Leyland Leopard for company.

Leeds City Council were very eager to promote the Leeds City Markets, which were facing some decline. Former WYPTE Olympian 5143 was chosen to carry the advert for the markets; it's seen here on Eastgate working the X11 short journey to Calverley.

New to Yorkshire Rider in 1988 is this MCW Metrobus 7592, which is carrying a rather optimistic advert for tape cassettes. The bus is seen on Briggate working the circular 2 Moortown to Middleton service, which is still operating today.

Yorkshire Rider – Building on a Great Tradition

Yorkshire Rider celebrated the former bus liveries of its operators across the years, with a special fleet of commemorative liveried vehicles. Former WYRCC 363, a Leyland National 2, pauses on Rouiger Street in full York West Yorkshire livery.

The darker pre-war Prussian blue livery used in Bradford until 1946 is illustrated on this former WYPTE Roe-bodied Leyland Olympian 5040. This vehicle was painted in 1986 to celebrate the sixtieth anniversary of Bradford motor buses. The livery stayed on 5040 with the addition of the Yorkshire Rider strap-line of 'Building on a great tradition'.

5117 another former WYPTE Olympian was repainted into the post-war lighter blue and cream livery that was used in Bradford after 1946 until March 1974. This scene has changed with the building of the long-overdue Broadway shopping mall.

For the 1987 Halifax depot opening, this 5096 – another former WYPTE Roe-bodied Olympian – was used to promote the day and celebrate seventy-five years of the motor bus within the Halifax area. Here the bus is seen departing Huddersfield on a short working of the 503 route to Bradford Interchange.

With the withdrawal of Northern Counties-bodied Leyland Fleetline 7006, the Todmorden livery was painted upon 5156, which was new in 1988. Here the bus is parked within the confines of the Halifax bus station in-between duties.

The York Corporation fleet was acquired by West Yorkshire RCC in 1934, which became the York West Yorkshire operation lasting until 1986. York City & District took over from the YWY network under new owner AJS Holdings, until purchase by Yorkshire Rider in July 1990. Former WYRCC Olympian 5196 pauses near Piccadilly in York in full Corporation blue livery, with stylish gold lining out.

In 1983 West Yorkshire PTE repainted this Roe-bodied Leyland Atlantean into a special livery, marking the centenary of Huddersfield transport from 1883 to 1983. 6299 carries the livery adapted for the traditional liveries fleet, as seen here in the Bradford Interchange. This bus currently survives as a canteen in the southern part of the UK.

Atlantean 6300 was also chosen to celebrate the Huddersfield centenary celebrations in this tramway livery, with lining out. Like 6299, this bus carried the livery until around 2001 when both were repainted into the First Huddersfield livery. At the time of writing 6300 is still undergoing restoration in West Yorkshire.

The Leeds one-man-operation livery was painted on MCW Metrobus 7575, which is seen on Sovereign Street in Leeds with a very happy crew on board. This bus was also used at Bramley bus depot for guided bus way trials on a small section installed within the depot yard.

Two former West Yorkshire RCC ECW-bodied Leyland Olympians were repainted into the Tilling red and cream era WYRCC livery – 5187 and as-shown 5199. This bus was 1863 in the West Yorkshire fleet (the last Olympian in the fleet) and is paused inside the original Bradford Interchange, working the 637 Clayton service.

Leyland Leopard with Plaxton Derwent bodywork 8534 was new to the PTE in 1976, with dual-purpose seating from new. Here the bus is collecting passengers from Keighley bus station for a trip out to Hebden Bridge – a popular tourist village. 8534 carried this Todmorden livery until withdrawn in 1999 by First; currently 8534 is preserved in the original WYPTE saloon livery.

Leyland Fleetline 7006, with low-height Northern Counties bodywork, was used to promote the Todmorden depot open in June 1987. The bus is painted into the Todmorden JOC livery celebrating eighty years of service in this posed picture. (**Malcolm King Collection**)

Leeds City Transport 591, a 1974-delivered Leyland Atlantean with Roe bodywork, which was placed straight into service on 31 March 1974. Like most of these former Leeds buses, which had passed to the new PTE in 1974, over 100 were taken into Yorkshire Rider stock. By 1993 the remaining handful were withdrawn due to new legislation regarding dual-door buses. However, three survive into preservation in various parts of Yorkshire – 560, 588 and 591.

Former PTE Leyland Leopard/Plaxton 8515 was transferred across to the newly acquired WYRCC fleet during 1989. Here this saloon is paused at Bradford Interchange before returning to Bingley on the 692 service.

Posed at Todmorden bus station is this special-liveried Freight Rover Sherpa 1870 with sixteen dual-purpose seat Dormobile bodywork. This vehicle was given the 'Magic Micro' name and it looks stunning in this overall black livery with Yorkshire Rider logos. (**Malcolm King Collection**)

A selection of Mk II Metrobuses had the rear end lower section altered with a smaller window and thicker strengthened surrounds. Here 7522 paused on Briggate shows off the new neater small lower saloon rear window.

West Yorkshire PTE used the new Leyland Tiger coach chassis for the private hire Metro Coach division. Here Jonckheere-bodied 1612 is parked in Leeds Central bus station, awaiting its next duty, in full Gold Rider livery. The coach gained its new registration during May 1988, the coach was new in 1985.

Leyland Atlantean 6058 with Charles H. Roe bodywork is depicted parked outside of the former 1937 Leeds Corporation tram depot on Torre Road. The depot suffered a fire in 1995, with the loss of some Atlanteans and Metrobuses. The bus depot was sold by First in 1996 and was demolished before being turned into a Ford Transit sales centre.

During 1994/5, Rider York won the contract from Stevenson's of Easingwold to run the then small park-and-ride services using a batch of Wright Axcess-Ultralow-bodied Scania saloons, with 8408 illustrated on Rougier Street in York. York still operates the park-and-ride services using articulated and electric powered vehicles.

Rider York also gained a batch of five Alexander Strider-bodied Scania L113CRLs, which arrived during 1994. Here 8404 pauses on Rougier Street to collect passengers for a trip to Poppleton, a village outside of York.

During the final year of operating the remaining Leeds City Atlanteans, most were found on the cross-city service 57 between Ireland Wood and Swacliffe, the 71 Primley Park to Bradford and the 41 Bramley depot to Seacroft. Here 581 turns into Albion Street off the Headrow in Leeds, bound for Ireland Wood.

This Northern Counties-bodied Daimler Fleetline was new to the Halifax Joint Omnibus Committee in 1972. Here 3305 is paused between duties on the 592 service at Todmorden bus station, with PTE livery and Yorkshire Rider vinyls. (**Malcolm King Collection**)

Following from the West Yorkshire RCC purchase from August 1989 that saw the fleet fully absorbed in April 1990, here Bristol VRT 741 is paused in Hall Ings, Bradford, not long after transfer to the Bradford Hall Ings bus depot.

One of fifty-five Scania L113 chassis delivered with Alexander Strider bodywork arrived in 1994, with the batch split in two, the first thirty-five in Yorkshire Rider livery. However, 8635 was quickly repainted into the Rider SuperBus livery, as illustrated by 8650 seen on Vicar Lane, Leeds. The Superbus used a small 500-metre section of guided busway on Scott Hall Road for services working the Scott Hall Road routes of the 35, 45, 48 and 71.

For the new deliveries of Volvo B10B and Scania L113 saloons, Yorkshire Rider worked with Alexander of Falkirk, producing the Strider style of bodywork. Here Scania 8615 is seen on the Headrow working a Sunday service to Wetherby during the summer of 1995.

A former York-West Yorkshire ECW-bodied Leyland Olympian is seen on Bridge Street, Bradford, while on a short transfer to the city. The bus later returned to York to finish her days, being withdrawn in November 2006.

Metrobus 7534 was chosen for a special livery to promote the Leeds Art Gallery, which was having a large promotional push during 1998. Here the bus is paused on City Square near the Mill Hill chapel. You can also see the NatWest building with overhead walkway that allowed pedestrians to cross the busy Park Row. (**David Longbottom Collection**)

The festive season saw Yorkshire Rider continue with the WYPTE tradition of making special Christmas buses. Four vehicles were chosen – 6240, 6262, 6304 and 6263, as illustrated above. This festive Atlantean pauses on Briggate, sporting *Dancer* name and illuminated advert panels. (**Malcolm King Collection**)

Atlantean 6262 is posed at Sovereign Street depot sporting the full festive livery and *Prancer* name. This vehicle was used to promote the 1983 *Bus Fayre* open days at Kirkstall and Middleton depots, in an overall yellow livery with 'off-peak' letters advertising the new low fares on weekdays and weekends. (**Malcolm King Collection**)

6020 was to be the final former WYPTE standard Atlantean with Roe bodywork to be in the former PTE livery. Here the bus pulls away from a stop on Sunbridge Road in Bradford, during 1990. This bus was withdrawn and later became the tree lopper bus among other uses.

After leaving the Kirkstall Road works, 6020 emerged as the tree lopper 9339, initially with large Yorkshire Rider fleetnames on the lower panels. Here 9339 is seen parked up with the workforce trimming the many trees along a bus route. The bus also doubled as a driver training unit and a football special ticket office. (**Malcolm King Collection**)

The batch of fifteen Optare-bodied Leyland Cub minibuses, derived from the Leyland terrier truck chassis, had a short life with Yorkshire Rider; all were withdrawn by July 1987. Here 1804 is posed in Halifax Skircoat Road depot in full Yorkshire Rider livery. (**Malcolm King Collection**)

West Yorkshire PTE purchased several batches of Freight Rover Sherpa minibuses in the lead up to deregulation. Fifteen examples were bodied by Optare, Cross Gates, Leeds. Here 1701 is posed for an official photograph, in full Micro Rider livery. (**Malcolm King Collection**)

1714, another of the Optare-bodied Freight Rover Sherpa minibuses, pauses outside of the Leeds Lewis store on the Headrow, heading for Seacroft. Like the Optare-bodied Leyland Cubs, the minibuses were withdrawn during May/June 1987. (**David Longbottom Collection**)

The standard Dormobile-bodied bread van chassis for the initial batches of minibuses ordered by the PTE, but operated in service by Yorkshire Rider. Here 1786 is parked up in the former Kings Cross Halifax bus station, awaiting its next duty. (**David Longbottom Collection**)

This former WYPTE Atlantean was decorated as one of the Christmas vehicles during late 1987. 6240 is paused on City Square. Here the bus is seen working the late-night Night Rider service 920 to Lawnswood as *Dancer*, one of the reindeer who help Santa at Christmas. (**Malcolm King Collection**)

Headingley-based 6304 collects passengers on Briggate during the Christmas season on the special 100 service for shoppers. Like 6240, 6304 has an illuminated side advertisement panel. All four Atlanteans were used as the Christmas buses, 6240, 6262, 6263 and 6304, each carrying the names *Dancer*, *Donner*, *Prancer* and, of course, *Rudolf* – the one with the red nose. (**Malcolm King Collection**)

Leyland Fleetline 7007 with low-height Northern Counties bodywork is seen in its home town, Todmorden. The bus is working a special works service, taking Yorkshire Rider employees to and from the depot.

7073 became the last WYPTE Fleetline to be withdrawn from service in July 2001. Here the bus pauses at the 1995-built Halifax bus station, which won an award for its construction.

MCW's final new bus model was the integral MetroRider, which was a proper constructed minibus. Yorkshire Rider purchased forty examples between 1987 and 1988. Here 2035 is parked outside Sovereign Street depot, having competed a full day in service.

MCW MetroRider 2020 was one of five delivered in 1987 with dual-purpose coach seats and in full Gold Rider livery. The bus is seen in Huddersfield working the service to Dalton while in use at Huddersfield depot.

Following the sake of the MCW Metrobus and MetroRider to Leeds-based Optare, the MetroRider was placed direct into production with a few tweaks by Optare. Here, posed on Swinegate, Leeds, is the demonstrator delivered to Yorkshire Rider. It was used in service, but no orders were placed. (**Malcolm King Collection**)

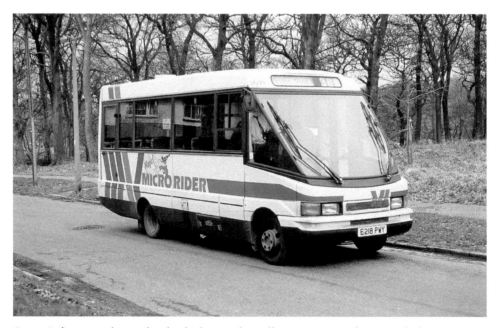

Optare's first complete stylised vehicle was the Volkswagen LT55 chassis with the City Pacer bodywork. Yorkshire Rider purchased fifteen examples during 1987, with 2019 being exhibited at the annual Coach & Bus Show. These new minibuses were launched at the Queen's Hall in Leeds prior to entering service. (**Malcolm King Collection**)

This former Rhodes Coaches East Lancashire-bodied Scania K92, new in 1987 and acquired by Yorkshire Rider in 1994. The bus became 8600 and is seen on the Headrow working the peak-time X11 Leeds–Bradford service.

The Leyland Tiger Royal Doyen with Roe bodywork was Leyland's answer to the European coaches on the market at the time. WYPTE purchased 1603 in 1983 as part of the W. R. & P. Bingley operation. Here the coach is seen in Leeds being used as the Leeds United team coach. It was withdrawn and sold in May 1988. (**Malcolm King Collection**)

Yorkshire Rider purchased twenty-three former Greater Manchester standards, two with Park Royal bodies, the others having Northern Counties bodywork. 6401 with Park Royal bodywork is seen crossing Vicar Lane into the Headrow on a former West Yorkshire RCC service to Otley.

Former Leeds City Atlanteans 508–517 were transferred to the Kingsley depot upon closure of the Sovereign Street depot, which became the minibus depot. Here 514 is paused in Wakefield bus station, in PTE livery and Rider vinyls. Later, 514 would be purchased by Black Prince of Morley. (**David Longbottom Collection**)

Roe-bodied Leyland Olympian 5022 was new to Halifax in 1982 and the bus is seen in Halifax working the 575 Migley service. 5022 would last until being withdrawn and sold for scrap in 2004. (**David Longbottom Collection**)

In 1994, Bristol-based Badgerline acquired the whole Yorkshire Rider operation; this was finally completed in March 1994. The next new vehicles ordered for operation in Yorkshire were the Dennis Dart and Lance, most with Plaxton bodywork and some with Alexander bodies. Here 4016 a Plaxton/Dennis is seen in Huddersfield having returned from Oldham.

Leeds were given all the Alexander Dash-bodied Dennis Darts, numbers 3219–3268, in the new Rider livery. Here 3268 is seen on Briggate before the street became pedestrianised, working its way to Morley on the 51 service.

Huddersfield and Halifax had delivered the first of the new Plaxton Beaver-bodied Mercedes Benz minibuses. Like the initial batches of the new Badgerline vehicles, the 22XX series were also painted into the new Rider livery.

The first eighteen Dennis Darts had Plaxton bodies and were new to Huddersfield in 1995. Here 3202 loads passengers for a duty to Bradley on the 321 service, after a drop of rain.

Yorkshire Rider
Driver Training Units

Halifax Corporation Leyland Titan, which passed to the WYPTE in 1974 and then became a driver training unit. It later passed to Yorkshire Rider. 9345 pauses within Halifax bus station having done a training duty on 1 August 1990.

Ordered by Huddersfield Corporation, a batch of Roe-bodied Fleetlines were delivered to the PTE. As 4167 this bus worked all its life with the PTE, passing to Yorkshire Rider in 1986. Here as trainer 9372, the bus is parked in Leeds Central bus station, in company with two West Riding vehicles.

A former Leeds City Atlantean is parked at the Bradford Interchange while taking another recruit around the local area. 9377 was sold to Pocklington Gliding School outside of York and later preserved.

Another former Leeds Atlantean stands outside the Sovereign Street training depot as 9375, awaiting another turn. The driving school was later transferred to Bramley depot when Sovereign Street was closed.

During 1994, Yorkshire Rider had to replace the double-deck training fleet, after new rules were introduced. Here 9413, a former Barton coach, is kindly paused by the driving instructor on New York Street, before continuing to another training duty.

After a few years as single-deckers on the training fleet, several former PTE Atlanteans were converted to driver trainers. Here 9281, formerly 6129, pauses at Huddersfield bus station while in service.

Another view of 9372, this time paused outside of the Leeds Sovereign Street depot, which at the time was the home of the training school. (**Malcolm King Collection**)

The two classic Leyland Titan with Roe bodies are seen together at the Halifax depot open day on 14 June 1987. 9345 and 9346 were the last Halifax vehicles to be withdrawn by Yorkshire Rider during 1991. (**David Longbottom Collection**)

9376 was seen wandering around the hilly environs of Halifax, again while on training duty. This former Leeds City Atlantean was the final dual-door bus to be withdrawn by Yorkshire Rider in July 1993.

Demonstrators and Rare Workings

Before joining its owners, Preston Bus, this all-Leyland Olympian was demonstrated to Yorkshire Rider. Here the bus is parked in Leeds bus station lay-over bay awaiting a return to Halifax on the 508 service.

This former Leeds Atlantean was withdrawn in November 1986 to be converted into the Yorkshire Rider Roadshow bus and was used as such from May 1987. The bus was used at the depot open days, as seen here with it outside the Halifax Skircoat Road depot. The bus was later reregistered as AN231M and sold to Leeds City Council. (**Malcolm King Collection**)

The Leyland Lynx integral city bus was the next vehicle to replace the Leyland National; it entered production in 1986. Yorkshire Rider tried this example seen here on Briggate, Leeds, working the 23 Gledhow–Middleton service. (**Malcolm King Collection**)

Another Leyland Lynx demonstrator is seen in Swinggate/Sovereign Street depot, awaiting trials in service. No orders for the Lynx were placed by Yorkshire Rider. (**Malcolm King Collection**)

The Talbot Express van chassis was tried by a handful of operators; here this example is seen working with Yorkshire Rider. The bus is depicted working the 66 service to Old Farnley, running along Hall Lane. (**Malcom King Collection**)

Carlyle in Birmingham had improved on the initial bread van style of bodywork with its Mk II version, which had around twenty-plus seats. Here in Swinggate depot are the two former demonstrators; they were new in August 1987 and entered service after trials in early 1988. (**Malcolm King Collection**)

An unusual mix of Carlyle Mk II bodywork on an Iveco 49:10 chassis is this member of the Micro Rider fleet. 2060 is seen operating the 66 service to Leeds bus station. (**Malcolm King Collection**)

Already seen within this volume is 1717 at the Bradford Interchange. Here the bus is seen in the demonstration livery of Carlyle works. (**Malcolm King Collection**)

A quartet of demonstrators within the Sovereign Street depot – a GMBuses Little Gem, a Mk II Carlyle Sherpa, a Robin Hood-bodied Sherpa, and sneaking into the picture is a former West Midland PTE Carlyle-bodied Sherpa. (**Malcolm King Collection**)

A closer look at the unusual mixture of the Freight Rover Sherpa chassis with a Robin Hood City Nippy body. This vehicle is seen in Sovereign Street depot, awaiting use in a trials and passenger feedback survey. (**Malcolm King Collection**)

For trials of a guided busway in Leeds, a small section was constructed at Bramley depot for extensive testing. Here Leeds City Transport-liveried MCW Metrobus 7575 is seen undergoing tests on the track. A 500-metre section was built on Scott Hall Road and promoted as the 'Super Busway', opening in 1995. (**Malcolm King Collection**)

Yorkshire Rider also tried an Optare Delta/DAF SB250LC demonstrator along the test track at Bramley. Five of this vehicle type were ordered for 1989 delivery, in Yorkshire Rider livery and used on the 8 and 9 ring-road services. (**Malcolm King Collection**)

The Leyland Cubs with Optare bodywork were the regular vehicles on the 66 Leeds bus station–Pudsey–Greengates service. Here 1813 is seen departing the original Pudsey bus station for Leeds. (**Malcolm King Collection**)

1811, another Leyland Cub/Optare midibus, is seen working the 700 Bradford shop hopper service from the Interchange forecourt. The bus has Yorkshire rider vinyls applied over the PTE livery. (**Malcolm King Collection**)

Roe-bodied Atlantean 6221 is seen at the Corn Exchange stops in full Yorkshire Rider livery, sporting an advert for the Micro Rider minibuses. (**David Longbottom Collection**)

Optare-bodied VW LT55 1700 is seen on Wellington Street, Leeds, in full Gold Rider livery; this was the one City Pacer to be in this livery. It was new in April 1987 and withdrawn in March 1990, but it has been preserved and is currently with the Dewsbury Bus Museum Collection. (**David Longbottom Collection**)

Yorkshire Rider began to develop a holiday programme for passengers and holidaymakers alike. Here Alexander-bodied Scania N113DRB 8014 is posed in Middleton to promote the new Rider travel shop in Leeds. (**Malcolm King Collection**)

Seen posed at a rather damp Sovereign Street minibus depot is this smart looking Mercedes-Benz 811D minibus with Reeve Burgess bodywork. It was new to Traject Halifax in late 1988 and is seen here in full Gold Rider livery. (**Malcolm King Collection**)

Former Bradford Fleetline 2342 was reinstated into the Yorkshire Rider fleet at Huddersfield from late 1986 until June 1988. Here the bus is seen loading for a trip on the 370 service to Rawthorpe. This was the only Alexander-bodied Bradford Fleetline to serve with Yorkshire Rider, as 2345, which was based in Halifax, had a 1974 Northern Counties body. (**Malcolm King Collection**)

With the purchase of the former West Yorkshire RCC and York City & District operations came several Iveco 49:10 TurboDaily with Robin Hood City Nippy bodies. 2072 is one such example, which is seen on the Interchange forecourt on shopper's service 600. The minibus was also freshly repainted into the Micro Rider livery.

2012, a Reeve Burgess-bodied Mercedes-Benz L608D minibus that was new to Eastern National, was transferred to Yorkshire in 1994 to combat a new operator in Huddersfield. Here the bus, in full Yorkshire Rider saloon livery, is seen departing Huddersfield on the 819 service.

8653 is seen heading down the Headrow while operating slightly off-route on the cross-city 57 service between Ireland Wood and Barwick, in full Superbus livery, which was a smartly turned out style.

Atlantean 6050 is paused at the Jacob's Well bus stop, just off the roundabout, while working the 641 Shipley service. In the windscreen is the quick fare exact fare sticker, a system used to improve dwell times at bus stops as passengers tendered the exact fare.

An elevated view of Atlantean 6205 seen inside the old proper Bradford Interchange while on 636 duty. A walkway from Nelson Street to Norfolk Gardens allows people to pass through the bus station.

6063 was one of twenty-two Leeds-based Roe-bodied Leyland Atlanteans transferred across to Halifax before the start of deregulation. The bus is seen in the old Halifax bus station in Kings Cross. (**David Longbottom Collection**)

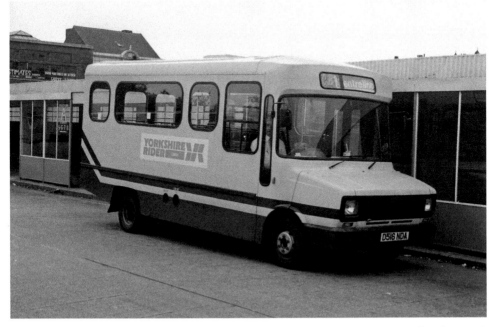

1916 a Carlyle-bodied Sherpa – one of twenty-five examples new to West Midlands Travel, acquired in 1987. It is seen working the CB1 centreline minibus service, which ran clockwise to and from the city rail station. (**David Longbottom Collection**)

An early PTE Atlantean seen working in Bradford on the 620 service to Bierley, near the St Johns Market centre.

Atlantean 6146 is seen about to depart Braford Interchange as it heads for Holme Wood estate on the northern side of the city, on the 618 service.

Scania N113 with Alexander bodywork, 8020, collects a passenger at the City Square stops before turning left into Infirmary Street, then into East Parade and on to Alwoodley.

8039 is seen in Bradford on Sunbridge Road while working a former West Yorkshire RCC service – the 655. This route goes via Shipley, Guiseley, Yeadon, West Park and into Leeds via Kirkstall Road.

Before the PTE had to suspend operating bus services in the new commercial era, two batches of five Optare-bodied Olympians (under licence from Leyland) were purchased. 5146, one of two convertible open-top buses, paused in Leeds bus station while on the 33 service.

York-based Wright-bodied Scania 8416 is seen in the city centre, in an overall white livery with Park and Ride vinyls. These new Scania saloons arrived in 1995–96 and were the first dedicated park-and-ride vehicles. Today the service has grown, using Mercedes-Benz articulated and Optare electric-powered vehicles.

8515, which was transferred across to the West Yorkshire RCC fleet during 1989 and painted in the Tilling Red livery. After some time 8515 returned to service, having been repainted into the 1990 revised Yorkshire Rider saloon livery. The bus is depicted in Halifax, after your author had travelled on the bus from Leeds.

8007 is seen pausing in Leeds Central Bus Station while employed on the 11 Bradford Road service. This vehicle is still going strong and earning its keep with ConneXions Buses of Tockwith.

An elevated view of Scania 8040, taken from the walkway that started from the NatWest bank on Park Row. It continued into Infirmary Street and, as can be seen, allowed for some interesting views of Leeds buses.

Huddersfield-based 7120, a Roe-bodied Leyland Fleetline, is seen departing the bus station in Huddersfield during the early 1990s – long before the introduction of all the traffic lights and crossing points.

Atlantean 6307 is seen working a former West Yorkshire RCC service, the 784 limited stop to Skipton. The bus turns into Albion Street from the Headrow as it heads out of Leeds. Today the route continues as the X84, using state-of-the-art low-floor vehicles.

Leeds Atlantean 586 is seen parked up in Leeds Central bus station before taking up duties on regular haunt, the 57, to Ireland Wood. These dual-door buses were used regularly Monday to Friday from 1986 until 1993.

Preserved Yorkshire Rider Buses

6020, which was converted into a tree lopper in 1991, became a driver trainer and the football special ticket office. It was preserved in April 2005 and from 2009 underwent a major restoration until it returned in 2015, as seen here in Bradford looking in fine fettle.

1700 – the Optare City Pacer-bodied VWLT55 van chassis is the only Yorkshire Rider vehicle of this type preserved. It's seen here posed at the 2013 Dewsbury Bus Museum spring open day; a Magic Micro Rider in Gold Rider livery.

8601 has been in preservation since 2008 and it was returned to preservation after a change of owners. Here the bus leaves Ravensthorpe after a busy day attending the spring Dewsbury Bus Museum open day.

This Optare-bodied Leyland Olympian is seen at Temple Newsam grounds while celebrating the bus's 25th anniversary. 5507 also returned home to Optare at Cross Gates, where it was built in 1986.

Acknowledgements

Sometimes things just fall into place with a little serendipity, which is the best way to describe this engagement. For those who know me, buses have been very much a part of life since the early days of my childhood. Having travelled on many an Atlantean, Fleetline, Olympian and Metrobus, surely the interest followed, as it did.

I'd like to thank the people at Amberley who approached the idea about a book about Yorkshire Rider buses. A few e-mails later and it's been commissioned, all by the end of November 2016.

Here I'd also like to thank Malcolm King – a long-time friend and fellow photographer and who was the official Yorkshire Rider photographer – for allowing me to use some truly great archive photos of the buses.

Next to thank is David Longbottom, again a fellow photographer, who has kindly allowed me to use some of his work.

I'd like to thank my mother and brother, who across the years have wondered why I do what I do, but they have also supported the photography and looked at my photos, on the computer or as 35mm stills.

Finally, to all my fellow enthusiasts, friends and photographers who I have met across the years, a thank you to you all for viewing my photos on Flickr.

First West Yorkshire repainted a 2008 Volvo B7TL with WrightBus Gemini bodywork; it was dedicated as a fitting tribute to the late Brian Parkin, who passed away in early 2015. Brian will be remembered as a Leeds-based transport historian and editor of the various guises of *Metro Transport News*. Here (3)7674 works the 965 Weston circular service on its first day in service, 18 March 2015.